4
Ingredients
One Pot,
One Bowl

Also by Kim McCosker

4 Ingredients Christmas: Recipes for a Simply Yummy Holiday
Baby Bowl: Home-Cooked Meals for Happy, Healthy Babies and Toddlers

By Kim McCosker and Rachael Bermingham

4 Ingredients Gluten-Free
4 Ingredients

4
Ingredients
One Pot,
One Bowl

Rediscover the Wonders of Simple, Home-Cooked Meals

Kim McCosker

ATRIA PAPERBACK

New York   London   Toronto   Sydney   New Delhi

ATRIA PAPERBACK

A Division of Simon & Schuster, Inc.
1230 Avenue of the Americas
New York, NY 10020

First Atria Paperback edition February 2013

ATRIA PAPERBACK and colophon are trademarks of Simon & Schuster, Inc.

For information about special discounts for bulk purchases,
please contact Simon & Schuster Special Sales at
1-866-506-1949 or business@simonandschuster.com.

The Simon & Schuster Speakers Bureau can bring authors
to your live event. For more information or to book an event,
contact the Simon & Schuster Speakers Bureau at
1-866-248-3049 or visit our website at www.simonspeakers.com.

Manufactured in China

10 9 8 7 6 5 4 3 2 1

Library of Congress Cataloging-in-Publication Data is available.

ISBN 978-1-4516-7803-1
ISBN 978-1-4516-7804-8 (ebook)

CONTENTS

Introduction

Back in 2006, when I sat down to write my first 4 Ingredients cookbook, my goal was to create for all of you what I wanted for myself: a simple guide to making home-cooked meals for my family. What could be easier than recipes that require only four or fewer ingredients? I'm not one to brag (really!), but seven years and five books later, I have to say I've outdone myself. *One Pot, One Bowl* is a glorious collection of sweet and savory dishes full of fresh, easy-to-find ingredients—no more than four in each recipe—that require only one pot and one bowl. That means less cleanup and more time enjoying these fabulous meals with the friends and family you love.

In this book, full of gorgeous photographs by Stuart Quinn, you will find recipes for casseroles, roasts, soups and stews, pizza, pasta, pies, and desserts. Some of my personal favorites are the Creamy Bacon & Sun-Dried Tomato Chicken, the French Lamb Casserole, the Apple Crumble, and the Baked Rice Pudding. That said, everything in these pages makes my mouth water, and I know yours will, too!

It is my intention with this cookbook to help every home chef rediscover the wonders of quick, easy, and delicious home-cooked meals. I truly hope you find some inspiration and a bit of kitchen wisdom within.

Happy cooking!

Kim

In the Cupboard

4 Ingredients One Pot, One Bowl offers a wide range of yummy recipes. However, as we tested and retested each one, we began to notice a pattern in the ingredients we called upon. What we aim to do in this section is help you stock your kitchen pantry, fridge, and freezer with the items you'll need to make the wonderful recipes throughout. In all likelihood, you have at least four of the ingredients below and you'll be well on your way to preparing anything in this book!

Please note: Salt, pepper, and water are not included in the four ingredients.

Pantry	Fridge and Freezer
Apple juice	Butter
Bananas	Cheeses: blue, Cheddar, feta, Jarlsberg, mozzarella, Parmesan, ricotta
BBQ sauce; enchilada sauce; ketchup; salsa	Cream cheese
Black olives	Eggs
Broths: beef, chicken, vegetable	Heavy cream
Canned beans: butter beans, chickpeas (garbanzos), red kidney	Milk
Canned dulce de leche	Sour cream
Canned fruit: apple pie filling, apricots, sliced peaches	Yogurt: plain, fruit-flavored
Canned tomatoes: diced, whole peeled	Refrigerated pie crusts
Capers	Mayonnaise
Chocolate: dark and milk	Prepared basil pesto

Pantry	Fridge and Freezer
Coconut milk	Bacon
Condensed soups: cream of asparagus, cream of celery, cream of chicken, cream of mushroom, cream of tomato, tomato	Fully cooked chorizo
Cream-style corn	Smoked salmon
Dried fruit: cranberries, raisins	Bell peppers: red, green
Dry soup mixes: onion, vegetable	Carrots
Flour: self-rising, all-purpose	Fresh herbs: cilantro, parsley, rosemary, sage, thyme
Honey; maple syrup	Fresh red chiles
Kecap manis; soy sauce*	Garlic
Muesli (fine granola); old-fashioned rolled oats	Lemons
Nutella (or similar chocolate-hazelnut spread)	Limes
Olive oil	Scallions (green onions)
Onions	Tomatoes: cherry, plum, regular, sun-dried
Pasta and egg noodles	Frozen puff pastry sheets
Pasta sauces	Frozen strawberries
Peanut butter	Frozen vegetables: peas, chopped spinach, mixed vegetables
Potatoes: russet (baking), Yukon Gold (boiling)	

*These ingredients can be found in the Asian foods section.

Breakfasts & Brunches

Rise and shine,
it's breakfast time!

Bacon & Egg Pie

f *Recipe from Shane Hunia of Coromandel, New Zealand.*

Serves 4

2 sheets frozen puff pastry, thawed
½ white onion, finely diced
4 slices bacon, coarsely chopped
6 large eggs

Preheat the oven to 400°F. Line a 10-inch quiche dish with parchment paper. Fit 1 sheet of puff pastry into the dish. Sprinkle with the onion and then the bacon. Crack the eggs into the dish without breaking the yolks, evenly covering the entire surface. Season generously with sea salt and pepper. Top with the second sheet of pastry. Roll the top edges together and, using a fork, seal the edges. Pierce the top crust 4 times with a fork. Bake for 25 minutes, or until puffed and golden.

Flowerpot Pesto Damper Bread

Traditionally, damper is made of flour, salt, and water kneaded into a thick bread-like mixture and cooked over an open fire in a rustic iron pot. Here is my tasty version, cooked in cute flowerpots!

Serves 4

> 1½ cups self-rising flour, plus extra for dusting
> 2 tablespoons butter, diced
> ⅔ cup milk
> 3 tablespoons prepared basil pesto

Preheat the oven to 375°F. In a large bowl, combine the flour with ½ teaspoon salt. Add the butter and rub into the flour with your fingertips until it resembles fine crumbs. Stir in the milk and pesto to form a soft dough. Turn onto a lightly floured surface and shape the mixture into four equal balls. Flour the insides of four, clean 5-ounce clay flowerpots. Fit one ball of dough into each pot, pressing it down lightly. Bake for 20 minutes, or until risen and lightly golden.

Tip: If you don't have any CLEAN flowerpots, use rinsed-out cans instead—cans from condensed soups work really well.

Huevos Rancheros

Serves 6

2 cans (14 ounces each) diced tomatoes with onions and garlic
2 red bell peppers, cut into strips
2 fresh red chiles, seeded and chopped
6 large eggs

In a large nonstick skillet, warm the tomatoes over medium heat. Add the bell peppers and chiles and cook until tender. Reduce the heat and simmer for 5 minutes. Season to taste with sea salt and pepper. Use a spoon to make six small wells in the sauce and carefully crack an egg into each well. Cover and poach the eggs for 3 to 4 minutes.

Optional: Add smoked paprika and bay leaves for extra flavor (remember to remove the bay leaves before serving!). Serve with warmed tortillas or toast.

Lemon Butter

A delicious spread for breakfast on warm toast. Or make a plain muffin batter, fill the muffin cups halfway, divide the lemon butter among them, then top with the rest of the batter and bake.

Makes approximately 1 cup

8 tablespoons (1 stick) butter
½ cup sugar
3 eggs, well beaten
Juice of 3 lemons

In a small saucepan, melt the butter. Add the sugar, eggs, and lemon juice. Cook over low heat, stirring constantly, until thick. Pour into a jar and store in the fridge.

Optional: Grate in the zest of 1 lemon. For passion fruit butter, omit the lemon zest and use ½ cup passion fruit pulp and ¼ cup lemon juice.

Hint: To make this in the microwave, melt the butter and sugar in a microwave-safe bowl. In a separate bowl, beat the eggs until frothy. Add the eggs and lemon juice to the butter mixture and microwave on medium-high for 5 minutes, stirring after each 1 minute of cooking.

Rise & Shine Oatmeal

This is a creamy, delicious, easy breakfast.

Serves 2

1 cup old-fashioned rolled oats
1½ cups milk
½ cup apple juice
½ cup dried cranberries

In a saucepan or microwave-safe bowl, combine the oats, milk, apple juice, and cranberries. Let the mixture sit overnight in the refrigerator. The next morning, warm the oatmeal on the stove or in the microwave.

Optional: Sprinkle with chopped nuts and wheat germ.

Salmon & Onion Omelets

Serves 4

8 eggs
¼ cup heavy cream
1 package (4 ounces) smoked salmon, torn into large pieces
4 scallions (green onions), whites finely chopped, greens sliced on an angle

In a large bowl, whisk the eggs and cream together. Season with sea salt and pepper to taste. Heat an 8-inch nonstick skillet over medium heat. Add the egg mixture, swirling the eggs quickly in a circular motion so they cook evenly. Once the eggs begin to set, drop the pieces of salmon and scallions over the top. Tilt the pan so that one side of the omelet folds over the other, then slide it out onto a cutting board. Cut into 4 wedges to serve.

Tip: Omelets are incredibly versatile. I love them filled with fresh spinach and feta; red and green bell peppers with finely chopped jalapeños; or mushrooms, tomatoes, and sharp Cheddar.

Strawberry Muesli Smoothie

Serves 4

    2 cups milk
    1 cup frozen strawberries
    ½ cup toasted muesli
    ½ cup fruit-flavored yogurt

Place all the ingredients in a blender and process until smooth.

Toasted Nutella Sammies

Now, I know this isn't much of a recipe, but every time I post this on our Facebook page, the feedback is amazing. It's really popular!

Serves 3

> 6 thick (½-inch) slices ciabatta bread
> ½ to ¾ cup Nutella or similar chocolate-hazelnut spread

Heat a grill pan over medium-high heat. Grill the bread until toasted, about 2 minutes per side. Spread the chocolate-hazelnut spread over 1 piece of toast. Top with the second piece of toast and serve.

Tip: Ciabatta (chah-BAH-tah), which in Italian means "slipper," is a long, flat, wide loaf of bread with a soft interior and a crisp, thin crust.

Snacks & Lunches

Make easy and soul-satisfying food with minimal fuss and quick cleanup.

These one-pot, one-bowl meals are perfect for lunches and snacks.

Most can be prepared ahead of time. Just store them in the fridge, reheat, and serve when unexpected guests arrive.

Basil Pesto Quiche

[f] *Such a lovely recipe from Clare Kill.*

Serves 6

1 sheet frozen puff pastry, thawed
5 eggs
½ to ⅔ cup prepared basil pesto, or 1 container (8 ounces) basil-based dip
1 cup shredded Cheddar cheese (4 ounces)

Preheat the oven to 350°F. Line a 10-inch quiche dish with a sheet of puff pastry (roll it out if necessary). Trim off excess pastry with a paring knife and turn the edge in on itself to form a rim. In a bowl, beat the eggs well. Stir in the pesto and half the Cheddar. Season to taste with sea salt and pepper. Pour the filling into the quiche dish and sprinkle with the remaining Cheddar. Bake for 35 to 40 minutes, or until set.

Optional: Add chopped olives and sun-dried tomatoes if you have any in your refrigerator.

Butternut Squash & Sage Quiche

Serves 6

½ pound butternut squash, peeled and cut into small chunks

1 container (15 ounces) ricotta cheese

3 eggs, lightly beaten

3 tablespoons fresh sage leaves

Preheat the oven to 400°F. Spread the squash in a 10-inch quiche dish and bake for 15 minutes, or until just tender. Remove the squash from the dish and let cool. Line the dish with parchment paper and return three-fourths of the roasted squash to it. In a bowl, whisk together the ricotta and eggs and season to taste with sea salt and pepper. Pour over the squash. Scatter the remaining squash and the sage around the top of the quiche. Bake until firm and golden, 35 to 40 minutes. Let cool before serving.

Tip: You can also make individual quiches in a muffin pan. The baking time will be about 15 minutes.

Chorizo & Pea Frittata

A colorful, golden frittata results when you make this recipe.

Serves 4

> 1 package (3.5 ounces) fully cooked chorizo, sliced
> ⅔ cup frozen peas, thawed and drained
> 4 eggs
> 2 ounces fresh mozzarella cheese, sliced

Preheat the broiler. In a nonstick skillet, cook the chorizo until golden, 3 to 4 minutes. Add the peas and cook in the chorizo oil for a few minutes. Season well with sea salt and pepper. In a bowl, whisk the eggs with a pinch of sea salt and pepper until you can no longer see any traces of egg white. Pour the eggs over the peas and chorizo and cook for 3 to 4 minutes, or until the eggs start to set around the sides of the pan. Dot the mozzarella over the top of the frittata. Put the pan under the broiler and cook until the frittata has set on top and the mozzarella has melted. Serve hot from the pan.

Homemade Chunky Fries

Serves 8

> 8 large russet (baking) potatoes
> ¼ cup all-purpose flour
> ¼ cup olive oil

Preheat the oven to 400°F. Line two baking sheets with parchment paper. Wash and peel the potatoes and cut them into chunky wedges, approximately ¾ inch wide. Place the flour into a large plastic bag and season with sea salt and pepper. Working in four batches, drop handfuls of the potato wedges into the bag and toss to coat. Remove and transfer to the baking sheets, placing the wedges in single file. Drizzle with the oil and turn to coat well. Roast for 50 to 60 minutes, or until crisp and tender.

[f] *Noeline Wright wrote: Add 1 envelope of vegetable soup mix to 1 cup of flour and use that to add a delicious flavor to your Homemade Chunky Fries.*

Optional: To make Chunky Cheese Chips, shred about 5 ounces Gouda cheese, to make 1¼ cups. When the potatoes are nearly finished roasting, top them with the cheese and return to the oven for 3 minutes so that the cheese melts.

Little Cheddar Pies

My entire family loves these!

Makes 12 pies

2 sheets refrigerated pie crust
4 eggs
1 cup heavy cream
1 cup shredded Cheddar cheese (4 ounces)

Preheat the oven to 400°F. Cut twelve 2-inch rounds out of the pastry and fit into the cups of a regular muffin pan. In a bowl, beat the eggs. Stir in the cream, three-fourths of the Cheddar, and sea salt and pepper to taste. Divide the mixture evenly among the cups and top with the remaining Cheddar. Bake until set, 15 to 20 minutes.

Optional: Add whatever finely chopped veggies or freshly chopped herbs your family will eat. They are lovely!

Roast Beef "Lasagna"

This makes a fabulous meal for lunch or dinner. I called it "lasagna" because of the buttery smoothness of the croissants . . . Just yummy!

Serves 4

5 large croissants, split in half lengthwise
14 ounces sliced cooked roast beef
1½ cups tomato pasta sauce
10 ounces feta cheese, sliced

Preheat the oven to 350°F. Lightly grease a 9-inch round baking dish. Make layers in the baking dish in this order: croissant slices, roast beef, pasta sauce, and feta, ending with feta and seasoning with sea salt and pepper. Bake for 20 to 25 minutes to heat through.

Satay Chicken

Serves 4

1 teaspoon to 1 tablespoon red curry paste (depends on how much heat you like!)
1 pound skinless, boneless chicken breast halves, cubed
2 tablespoons peanut butter
¾ cup heavy cream

In a nonstick skillet, heat the curry paste. Add the chicken, stir to coat, cover, and let simmer for about 2 minutes. Add the peanut butter and cream, stir to combine, and simmer until the chicken is cooked, about 2 minutes more.

Optional: Serve atop rice or fettuccine and sprinkle with freshly chopped cilantro.
Toss in some thinly sliced vegetables if you have them in your fridge.

Tip: Red curry paste, a Thai ingredient, can be found in the Asian foods section.

Sloppy Joes

Serves 4

> 1 pound lean ground beef
> ¼ onion, chopped
> ¼ green bell pepper, chopped
> ¾ cup ketchup

In a nonstick skillet, brown the beef, onion, and green pepper over medium heat, stirring to break up the beef, then drain off any fat. Season with sea salt and pepper to taste. Stir in the ketchup and mix thoroughly. Reduce to a simmer and cook for 20 minutes.

Optional: My boys love this served up on hamburger buns.

Spinach Bread Bowl

Jocelyn Wilson told us that this was one of her family's favorites—it's now one of ours, too!

Serves 8

1 box (10 ounces) frozen spinach, thawed
1 container (16 ounces) sour cream
1 envelope vegetable soup mix
1 loaf (1 pound) round country bread or boule

Preheat the oven to 300°F. Squeeze the spinach dry and place in a large bowl. Stir in the sour cream and soup mix. Cut the top off the loaf and scoop out two-thirds of the bread inside, leaving a soft, plump wall. Pour the spinach mixture into the loaf and place on a baking sheet. Bake until lightly golden and crisp, about 20 minutes. In the last 6 minutes of baking, scatter the scooped-out bread chunks onto the baking sheet to toast. Serve on a platter using the "toast" to serve. Yummy!

Tip: Squeeze the spinach between paper towels.

Slow Cookers & Casseroles

Full of lean protein, hearty vegetables, and flavorful sauces, casseroles are the perfect option for a healthy dinner you can make ahead or serve the next day.

7-Minute Risotto

Serves 4 to 6

4 tablespoons (½ stick) butter
1 medium onion, diced
1½ cups Arborio rice
1 box (32 ounces) chicken broth

In a pressure cooker, melt the butter over high heat. Add the onion and cook until translucent. Add the rice and stir until nicely coated. Add the chicken broth and season with pepper. Lock the lid in place and cook over high heat for 3 minutes, or until steam emanates in a strong, steady stream. Reduce the heat to medium and cook for another 4 minutes. Remove from the heat and use the natural release method to unlock the lid. Stir and serve.

Optional: Add whatever veggies you want. Roasted beets and feta are lovely (as per the photo), as are peas and mushrooms. Sprinkle with grated Parmesan cheese and enjoy the quickest risotto you have ever cooked!

Beef & Potato Bake

Leftover roast beef plus three easy ingredients, and dinner is done!

Serves 4

> 4 medium potatoes, peeled and cubed
> 2½ cups chopped cooked roast beef
> 1 can (10.75 ounces) condensed tomato soup
> 2 cups shredded Cheddar cheese (8 ounces)

Preheat the oven to 350°F. In a 13 by 9-inch baking dish, combine the potatoes, beef, tomato soup, ¼ cup water (swirled in the soup can to rinse it), and sea salt and pepper to taste. Cover and bake until the potatoes are tender, about 1 hour. Uncover and sprinkle with the Cheddar during the last few minutes of baking so that the cheese melts into yummy goodness.

Tip: Any type of leftover meat can be used—barbecued chicken, lamb, pork, or ham.

Chicken Cacciatore

Cacciatore is an Italian dish of browned pieces of chicken covered in sauce with tomatoes, mushrooms, and onions. It's a very versatile dish and one you can make your own by adding peppers or other vegetables.

Serves 6

1 cup pitted black olives
6 skinless, bone-in chicken thighs
18 button mushrooms, washed
1 jar (24 ounces) chunky vegetable pasta sauce

Preheat the oven to 325°F. Heat a little of the oil from the olives in a large skillet over medium heat. Brown the chicken on all sides for about 10 minutes. Transfer the chicken to a large baking dish, add the mushrooms and olives, and season with sea salt and cracked black pepper. Pour the pasta sauce over the chicken, cover, and bake for 1½ hours, or until the chicken is fork-tender.

Optional: Serve over hot pasta and sprinkled with fresh parsley and Parmesan cheese . . . Yum scrum!

Chicken & Jarlsberg Casserole

The pairing of chicken and Jarlsberg in this recipe makes it a regular in my house. It's incredibly easy and full of glorious flavor.

Serves 6

6 skinless, boneless chicken breast halves
6 slices Jarlsberg cheese
1 can (10.75 ounces) condensed cream of chicken soup
¼ cup milk

Preheat the oven to 325°F. Place the chicken in an 8-inch square baking dish and cover with the cheese. In a small bowl, mix together the soup and milk. Pour the mixture over the casserole and bake for 1 hour, until the top is golden brown.

French Lamb Casserole

Simply put these four ingredients into a "bowl" for a meal bursting with flavor.

Serves 6

> 6 lamb shoulder chops (about 2 pounds)
> 1 envelope onion soup mix
> 1 can (14.5 ounces) diced tomatoes with herbs and garlic
> 6 carrots, halved crosswise

Place all the ingredients in a slow cooker and cook on low for 6 hours or on high for 3 to 4 hours.

Optional: Serve with mashed potatoes and steamed vegetables. Flowerpot Pesto Damper Bread (page 4) is divine with it, too!

Tip: Colors in slow-cooked food tend to fade, so garnish with something fresh and green when you serve.

Picante Chicken

Picante means "spicy" in Spanish, and this dish is definitely that. But it's a pleasant sweet spiciness that your entire family will love.

Serves 6

6 skinless, boneless chicken breast halves
2 cups salsa, your choice of hot or medium
⅓ cup light brown sugar
2 tablespoons honey-Dijon mustard

Preheat the oven to 350°F. Combine all the ingredients in a 13 by 9-inch baking dish. Bake until the chicken is thoroughly cooked, 40 to 45 minutes.

Optional: Add strips of red bell pepper before baking for added color and flavor.

Pulled Pork Sandwiches

Makes 8 fabulous sandwiches

    3 pounds boneless pork shoulder roast
    ⅔ cup apple cider vinegar
    1½ cups smoky barbecue sauce
    8 crusty rolls or hamburger buns

Trim excess fat from the pork roast. Sprinkle with sea salt. Place in a slow cooker and pour the vinegar over the roast. Cover and cook on low until the pork is fork-tender and pulls apart easily, 8 to 10 hours. Remove the roast from the cooker and shred the meat into small pieces. Discard the cooking liquid. Return the pork to the slow cooker and stir in the barbecue sauce. Continue to cook until warmed through, about 30 minutes. Split and toast the rolls or buns and fill with the meat and sauce.

Optional: Top with a little coleslaw for a southern flair. I guarantee you will make these again!

Red Wine Roast Beef

This is heavenly.

Serves 6

3 pounds boneless beef round
1 envelope onion soup mix
½ cup red wine (any you would drink)
⅓ cup balsamic vinegar

Place the roast in a slow cooker. Sprinkle with the soup mix and pour in the wine, vinegar, and ½ cup water. Cover and cook on low for at least 6 hours.

Optional: When the roast is finished cooking, pour the juices into a saucepan, heat over medium, and stir in 2 tablespoons cornstarch that has been mixed with a little cool water for a really flavorsome gravy!

Tip: Resist peeking! Every time the slow cooker lid is lifted, heat escapes and you'll need to add 15 to 20 minutes to the total cooking time.

Pots & Pans

These one-pot wonders have maximum flavor but require minimum preparation and cleanup.

Love 'em!

Beef Stroganoff

This is requested at least weekly in my house.

Serves 4

> 1 pound beef round, cut into thin strips
> 1 envelope beef stroganoff seasoning
> ½ package (8-ounce package) cream cheese, softened
> 1 package (8 ounces) mushrooms, sliced or quartered

Lightly brown the beef in a nonstick skillet. Add the seasoning with 1 cup water and simmer for 1 hour. Stir in the cream cheese until a nice, smooth sauce results. Add the mushrooms and simmer for a final 10 minutes.

Optional: Serve over rice to soak up the deliciously rich and inviting sauce.

Blue Cheese–Stuffed Pork with Pears

I am passionate about simplifying everyday cooking. I believe I have done just that with this gloriously easy dish!

Serves 4

4 thick pork rib chops
½ cup crumbled blue cheese (2 ounces)
1½ teaspoons butter
1 ripe pear, cored and sliced

Cut a horizontal slit through the thickest portion of each pork chop to form a pocket. Stuff 2 tablespoons blue cheese into each pocket. Season both sides of the pork with sea salt and pepper to taste. In a large nonstick skillet, cook the chops until cooked through but still juicy, about 3 minutes per side. Remove the chops from the pan. Add the butter to the pan and swirl to melt and coat the pan. Add the pear, season with sea salt and pepper to taste, and cook, stirring occasionally, until lightly browned, about 4 minutes. Serve the pork with the pear.

Optional: Serve with sautéed or steamed asparagus.

Bolognese Sauce

Serves 4

    1 pound ground beef
    1 can (14.5 ounces) diced tomatoes
    1 tablespoon dried Italian herbs
    1 cup beef broth

In a large saucepan, brown the ground beef over medium-high heat, stirring constantly to break up the meat, then drain off any fat. Add the tomatoes and their juices, the herbs, broth, and sea salt and pepper to taste. Bring to a boil, reduce the heat, and simmer for 45 to 55 minutes, or until most of the liquid has evaporated and the sauce remaining is nice and thick.

Tip: Cook once, eat twice! Make a double batch of this yummy sauce. Serve it over pasta one night. Then spread a sheet of puff pastry with the sauce, cover with fresh spinach and grated Parmesan cheese, roll, slice, and bake in a 400°F oven for 20 to 25 minutes, or until golden and puffed.

Chicken Tikka Masala

Here is my deliciously simple version of this classic Anglo-Indian dish!

Serves 4

3 skinless, boneless chicken breast halves, cut into chunks
2 tablespoons tikka masala paste
1 can (10.75 ounces) condensed cream of tomato soup
3 tablespoons plain yogurt

In a nonstick skillet, brown the chicken, 5 to 6 minutes. Add the tikka masala paste and soup and simmer for 15 minutes. Stir in the yogurt and heat through.

Optional: Serve with rice.

Tip: Tikka masala paste can be found with Indian ingredients in the Asian foods section.

Chili con Carne

I love this recipe . . . it allows me to cook once and eat twice! I double the recipe and serve it with rice one night, then spooned into a piping hot baked potato the next with a little sour cream and freshly grated Cheddar cheese.

Serves 4

> 1 pound lean ground beef
> 1 envelope chili con carne seasoning
> 1 can (14.5 ounces) diced tomatoes
> 1 can (15.5 ounces) red kidney beans, drained and rinsed

In a nonstick skillet, brown the ground beef over medium-high heat, stirring constantly to break up the meat, then drain off any fat. Stir in the seasoning, tomatoes, beans, and ½ cup water. Cover and simmer gently, stirring often, until the beef is cooked through, about 15 minutes.

Optional: We often add whatever vegetables we have in the fridge: onions, carrots, peppers, etc., as well as a hefty dollop of sour cream.

Corned Beef in Ginger Ale

Serves 6

    2½ pounds corned beef, in one piece
    1 bottle (1 liter) ginger ale

Place the meat in a large pot, add the ginger ale, cover, and cook until tender, about 1 hour.

Optional: Serve with a dollop of mango chutney, tomato relish, or mustard.

Tip: A general rule of thumb for corned beef is to allow 30 minutes per pound.

Creamy Bacon & Sun-Dried Tomato Chicken

🅕 *Melinda Dines wrote, "My family now has a new favorite meal. Thank you soooo much, 4 Ingredients!"*

Serves 4

6 slices bacon

4 skinless, boneless chicken breast halves, cut into wide strips

½ cup sun-dried tomatoes (drained if oil-packed), halved

1 tub (10 ounces) Philadelphia Cooking Creme (your choice of flavor)

In a nonstick skillet, cook the bacon until almost crisp. Add the chicken and cook, turning once, until cooked through and browned, 4 to 5 minutes. Drain off any excess fat. Add the tomatoes and sea salt and pepper to taste, and toss to combine. Add the creme and simmer until slightly thickened, 4 to 5 minutes.

Optional: Serve warm over a bed of rice, soft polenta, or mashed potatoes flavored with Parmesan cheese.

Garlic Cream Shrimp

A classic dish that is never outdated and is extremely popular on the 4 Ingredients Facebook page.

Serves 4

2 cups rice
2 cloves garlic, crushed through a press
½ cup heavy cream
16 jumbo shrimp, peeled and deveined

Bring a large saucepan of salted water to a boil, add the rice, and boil gently, stirring occasionally, for 12 minutes, or until tender. Drain, rinse under hot water, and drain again. In a small nonstick saucepan, heat the garlic in 1 tablespoon water for 30 seconds, or until just brown. Add the cream and bring to a simmer. Add sea salt and pepper to taste and let the sauce simmer and reduce for about 10 minutes. Add the shrimp and cook until they have turned pink, about 2 minutes. Serve on the rice.

Mussels in White Wine

This dish closely resembles moules marinières, *the national dish of Belgium, and is often served with French fries and homemade mayonnaise.*

Serves 4

2 tablespoons butter
1¼ cups white wine
3 pounds mussels, cleaned
2 tablespoons freshly chopped parsley

In a large pot, melt the butter. Pour in the wine and bring to a boil. Add the mussels, cover, and cook over medium heat, lightly shaking the pan every minute or so, until the mussels open, 4 to 5 minutes. Remove the mussels with tongs to a serving dish (leaving the liquid). Discard any mussels that are still closed. Bring the liquid in the pot to a boil. Season with sea salt and pepper and stir in the parsley. Pour the liquid over the mussels and serve immediately.

Optional: Add a little chopped scallion (green onion) to the mix.

Pork & Squash Curry

On the day of the photo shoot for this book, this dish actually silenced my mother—it was that tasty. My father has since asked for the recipe!

Serves 4

> 1 pound boneless pork (shoulder or loin), cubed
> 2 tablespoons red curry paste
> 1 can (13 ounces) coconut milk
> 1 pound butternut squash, peeled and cubed

In a large nonstick saucepan, brown the pork over medium heat. Add the curry paste and cook for 5 minutes. Add the coconut milk and ½ cup water to the pan. Add the squash, season with sea salt and pepper to taste, and bring to a boil. Reduce the heat and simmer until the pork and squash are cooked through, 30 to 40 minutes.

Optional: Serve with rice, lime halves to squeeze over, and a garnish of cilantro leaves and sesame seeds.

Tips: This is best made a few hours prior to serving, as it thickens as it cools. Simply reheat when ready to serve. Red curry paste, a Thai ingredient, can be found in the Asian foods section.

Sautéed Pork Chops with Chorizo & Tomato

When my beautiful sister-in-law, Nelly, first cooked this for me, I prayed it would never end! Serve on a bed of creamy mashed potatoes or sweet potatoes, and with greens.

Serves 6

6 thick pork rib chops (with or without bones)
1 fully cooked chorizo sausage, thinly sliced
1 pint cherry tomatoes
1½ cups chicken broth

In a large nonstick skillet, brown the chops on both sides. Remove from the pan and set aside. Add the chorizo to the pan and brown. Add the cherry tomatoes, toss with the chorizo, and fry for 3 minutes. Add the broth, stir well, and simmer for 3 minutes more. Return the pork to the pan and simmer in the sauce until the pork is tender and cooked through, about 10 minutes. Season with sea salt and cracked black pepper to taste.

Optional: Add 1 teaspoon smoked paprika, if you have it, when frying the chorizo.

Stilton Steak

Serves 2

    8 tablespoons (1 stick) butter, at room temperature
    2 tablespoons crumbled Stilton cheese (or other best-quality blue cheese)
    1 tablespoon port wine
    2 rib eye steaks

In a small bowl, beat the butter until smooth. Beat in the Stilton and port until well blended. Place the mixture on a small piece of parchment paper and roll into a ¾-inch cylinder; refrigerate. Season the steaks with salt and pepper and grill or broil to the desired doneness. Serve each steak topped with a slice of Stilton butter. Freeze the remaining butter for up to 3 months.

Optional: Serve with boiled potatoes and green beans.

Tip: To cook a great steak, heat a heavy-bottomed skillet over high heat before adding the oiled steak. This seals the surface, trapping in the juices. For medium doneness, cook a 2-inch steak for 4 minutes on each side. Transfer the steak to a plate, cover with foil, and set aside for 3 to 4 minutes. This allows the juices to settle and the muscle fibers to relax, which ensures an extra tender steak!

Sweet Chili Crab

Serves 2

> 1 cooked crab (about 2 pounds)
> ¾ cup sweet chili sauce
> Leaves from 1 bunch cilantro
> 2 cans (13 ounces each) coconut milk

Halve the crab and crack its claws. Put all the ingredients in a large saucepan, cover, and simmer over medium heat for 8 to 10 minutes, stirring occasionally, until the crab is heated through. Transfer to a serving plate and eat immediately with rice.

Tips: This dish can be made with any variety of crab or lobster. Sweet chili sauce is a Thai ingredient, different from regular tomatoey chili sauce; it's available in the Asian foods section and is a pantry staple in my house.

Tandoori Lamb Chops

Serves 4

½ cup tandoori paste
1½ cups plain yogurt
¼ cup coarsely chopped fresh cilantro
12 lamb rib chops, well trimmed

In a large bowl, combine the tandoori paste with half the yogurt and half the cilantro and coat the lamb with the mixture. Cover with plastic wrap and marinate in the refrigerator for 1 hour. Heat a nonstick skillet and cook the chops for 3 minutes on each side, or until cooked to your liking. Spoon on the remaining yogurt and sprinkle with the remaining cilantro.

Tip: Tandoori paste is an Indian ingredient, found in the Asian foods section.

Roasts & Bakes

[f] I asked our 4 Ingredients Facebook family,
"What is your family's favorite meal?"
The resounding answer was "A roast!"

Chicken Enchilada Cake

This is A.M.A.Z.I.N.G.L.Y. quick, easy, and delicious.

Serves 4

8 (8-inch) flour tortillas
1 can (10 ounces) enchilada sauce
2 cups shredded cooked chicken
1½ cups shredded mozzarella cheese (6 ounces)

Preheat the oven to 400°F. Line an 8-inch round cake pan with parchment paper. Make layers in this order: tortilla, sauce, chicken, mozzarella. Continue the layering process until all ingredients are used, ending with a layer of cheese. Bake until the cheese is completely melted and the sauce is bubbling, about 30 minutes.

Optional: If you'd like it a little moister, use 1½ cans of sauce, and if your family will eat them, add some beans or veggies for a little extra nutrition.

Easy Roast Beef

This is possibly my all-time favorite roast; you get the meal and the gravy in one dish!

Serves 4 to 6

2 pounds boneless beef rib roast, tied by the butcher
1 envelope onion soup mix
1 can (10.75 ounces) condensed cream of mushroom soup

Preheat the oven to 350°F. Place a large sheet of heavy-duty foil, enough to fully wrap the beef, in a roasting pan. Place the beef in the center of the foil and bring the foil up to make a bowl. In a small bowl, thoroughly mix the soup mix and canned soup. Pour over the beef and fold over the foil to seal tightly. Roast until tender, about 1 hour. Serve with the delicious gravy in the bottom of the pan and your family's favorite roasted veggies.

Feta & Capers in Baked Tomatoes

Serves 6

> 12 tomatoes
>
> 2 cups crumbled feta cheese (8 ounces)
>
> 3 tablespoons capers
>
> 1 egg, lightly beaten

Slice the top from each tomato. Scoop out the flesh and seeds with a teaspoon. Discard half (or freeze for another use) and place the rest in a bowl. Sprinkle the inside of each shell with a pinch of sea salt, turn upside down on paper towels, and leave to drain for 45 minutes. Preheat the oven to 325°F. To the tomato flesh, add the feta cheese and capers and mash until combined. Season with sea salt and pepper to taste. Beat in the egg until the mixture is thick and sticky. Turn the tomato shells upright, spoon in the cheese mixture, and replace the lids. Place the tomatoes in a baking dish that will hold them securely and bake for 10 minutes. Turn off the oven but do not remove the tomatoes for 5 minutes, then serve.

Honey-Baked Chicken

This dish is a marriage made in heaven and sensational served with small baked potatoes and seasoned beans sautéed in butter and lemon juice.

Serves 4 to 6

1 envelope onion soup mix
¾ cup white wine
3 tablespoons honey
2 pounds skinless, bone-in chicken pieces

Preheat the oven to 350°F. In a small bowl, combine the soup mix, wine, and honey. Arrange the chicken in a 9-inch baking dish and drizzle the wine mixture on top. Cover and bake for 1 hour. Uncover, reduce the temperature to 300°F, and bake for 30 minutes, or until golden and the chicken is cooked through.

Macaroni Bake

A recipe from the lovely Jenny Postle. Thanks, Jen.

Serves 4

> 4 cups cooked macaroni (about ½ pound uncooked)
> 1 can (10.75 ounces) condensed tomato soup
> ½ pound ham, cut into thin strips
> 1 cup shredded aged Cheddar or other sharp cheese (4 ounces)

Preheat the oven to 350°F. In a 13 by 9-inch baking dish, combine the macaroni, soup, ¼ cup water (swirled in the soup can to rinse it), and ham. Top with the cheese and bake for 20 minutes to heat through and melt the cheese.

Optional: Mix some freshly grated bread crumbs into the cheese topping.

Tip: Don't cook pasta all the way through before using it in a casserole; it will go mushy. Cook your pasta 2 to 4 minutes shy of the suggested cooking time on the package.

Roast Lamb

Serves 4

> 3 pounds semi-boneless leg of lamb (shank end)
> Leaves from 1 sprig rosemary
> 4 cloves garlic, sliced
> 2 tablespoons olive oil

Preheat the oven to 350°F. Cut ¾-inch slits in the lamb in several places and insert 6 rosemary leaves and 1 or 2 slices of garlic. Place the roast in a roasting pan, drizzle with the oil, season with sea salt and pepper, and roast for about 1½ hours, basting every half hour. To tell if the lamb is cooked to your liking, insert a skewer into the center, remove it, then press the flat of the skewer against the meat. As the juice runs out, you will see to what degree the meat is cooked—the pinker the juice, the rarer the meat.

Optional: Serve with roast vegetables and gravy. For a lovely variety, choose Yukon Gold potatoes, beets, carrots, Brussels sprouts, and butternut squash and drizzle with a mixture of olive oil, thyme, and rosemary. Season with sea salt and pepper and roast.

Tip: The golden rule for roasting lamb is to roast for 30 minutes per pound.

Roast Pork with Cherry Tomatoes

Serves 6

> 3 pounds boneless pork shoulder roast, rind on (see Tip), tied by the butcher
> 1 cup dry sherry
> ¼ cup maple syrup
> 1 pint cherry tomatoes

Preheat the oven to 400°F. Place the pork in a roasting pan and score the skin. Pour the sherry and maple syrup over the pork and season the skin generously with sea salt. Roast for 20 minutes, then reduce the heat to 325°F and roast for 1 hour. In the last 20 minutes of roasting, add the tomatoes. Let the pork rest for 10 to 15 minutes, then slice and serve with the tomatoes and pan juices.

Optional: Delicious served with creamy mashed potatoes.

Tip: In Australia, it's the rind that makes roast pork so popular . . . you might have to special-order from your butcher to get the rind, but it will be worth it!

Salt & Cumin Roast Chicken

Serves 4

> 3 pounds skin-on, bone-in chicken pieces
> 2 cups chicken broth
> 1 teaspoon ground cumin
> 2 tablespoons butter, melted

Preheat the oven to 400°F. Place the chicken pieces on a rack set over a large roasting pan. Pour the broth into the pan. Combine 2 teaspoons of sea salt with the cumin. Brush the chicken with the butter and sprinkle with the seasoning. Roast until cooked through, about 1 hour. Use the pan juices to dress the chicken when ready to serve.

Optional: Serve with a fresh garden salad dressed with a lovely vinaigrette.

Sausage Bake

So easy, so tasty, so cheap!

Serves 4

> 2 packages (12 to 14 ounces each) beef sausage
> 1 package (12 ounces) frozen country-style mixed vegetables, thawed
> 1 cup shredded Cheddar cheese (4 ounces)
> 1 can (10.75 ounces) condensed cream of mushroom soup

Preheat the oven to 300°F. Combine all the ingredients with ¼ cup water (swirled in the soup can to rinse it) in a baking dish and season with sea salt and pepper. Cover the dish and bake for 45 minutes. Uncover, stir, and bake for 15 minutes more, until browned on top.

Optional: I used a long rectangular (13 by 9-inch) baking dish, so my sausages browned. If you use a deeper casserole, you may want to brown your sausages lightly before baking. Maybe it's just me, but I like color in my sausages however they are cooked!

Sticky Pork Ribs

Serves 4

1 or 2 racks pork spareribs (3 to 4 pounds total)
¼ cup kecap manis
½ cup ketchup
½ cup barbecue sauce

Line a baking sheet with 2 layers of parchment paper and place the ribs on the baking sheet. In a bowl, combine the kecap manis, ketchup, and barbecue sauce. Pour over the ribs, turning to coat. Cover with plastic wrap and refrigerate for 2 hours. When ready to cook, preheat the oven to 350°F. Remove the plastic wrap and bake the ribs for about 50 minutes, turning and basting occasionally. To serve, cut between the ribs to separate.

Tip: Thick kecap manis is also known as "sweet soy sauce" and is available in the Asian foods section.

Topsi-Turnie Cake

Serves 4 to 6

> 1 large turnip or medium rutabaga, peeled and chopped
> 4 large russet (baking) potatoes, peeled and chopped
> 4 tablespoons (½ stick) butter, plus a little extra for greasing the pan
> 8 thin slices prosciutto

Preheat the oven to 350°F. In a saucepan of boiling salted water, cook the turnip and potatoes until fork-tender, 15 to 20 minutes. Drain and smash (leave them chunky) with half the butter and sea salt and pepper to taste. Grease an 8-inch round cake pan and line the bottom with prosciutto so that it fans out from the center like bicycle spokes. Press the veggies into the pan and dot with the remaining 2 tablespoons butter. Bake until crisp and golden, 40 to 45 minutes. Remove, let cool slightly, then turn out and cut into wedges to serve.

Tip: There are more than five hundred varieties of potatoes available to grow! The best variety for mashing are russet potatoes, Yukon Gold potatoes, round red or white potatoes, and purple potatoes.

Yummy Tuna Bake

This recipe was made by Harrison Dines, age ten. If your kids eat tuna, this is bound to become a fast and easy family favorite.

Serves 6

12 ounces egg noodles or cut pasta such as penne

1 can (12 ounces) tuna in water, drained

1 cup shredded Cheddar cheese (4 ounces)

1 can (10.75 ounces) condensed cream of celery soup

Preheat the oven to 350°F. Cook the noodles according to package directions but a little shy of being done. Drain and cool slightly. Transfer the noodles to a 9-inch baking dish, add the tuna, half the cheese, the soup, and ¼ cup water (swirled in the soup can to rinse it), and season with pepper to taste. Sprinkle with the remaining cheese. Bake until the cheese is bubbling, about 30 minutes.

Optional: Add ½ cup each of peas and corn kernels before baking.

Soups & Stews

Soups and stews are both satisfying and easy to whip up.

Literally take four simple ingredients and simmer until tender. What could be easier?

Bacon & Pea Soup

All the flavor of traditional pea and ham soup, but with a fraction of the effort, time, and money.

Serves 4

¾ pound thick-cut bacon, chopped
1 onion, coarsely chopped
3⅓ cups frozen peas, thawed (reserve a few for garnish)
1 box (32 ounces) vegetable broth

In a large saucepan, fry the bacon until golden. Set aside some for garnish. Move the rest to the side and in the fat gently fry the onion until just translucent. Add the peas and vegetable broth. Bring to a boil, reduce to a simmer, and cook until the peas are tender, 3 to 5 minutes. Using a handheld blender, blend the soup until smooth. To serve, pour the soup into bowls and garnish with a few whole peas and a little crispy bacon.

Chorizo & Chickpea Stew

A cozy, warm stew whipped up with minimal fuss . . . my favorite kind!

Serves 4

> 5 to 6 ounces fully cooked chorizo, thickly sliced
> 1 pint cherry tomatoes
> 1 can (15 to 16 ounces) chickpeas, rinsed
> 2 cups chicken broth

Heat a deep pot and brown the chorizo, about 2 minutes. Add the tomatoes, chickpeas, and broth. Bring to a boil, reduce to a simmer, and cook for 15 minutes. Season with sea salt and pepper to taste.

Optional: An ideal accompaniment is a quick, creamy polenta made by simply adding cornmeal to boiling water, whisking until absorbed, then stirring in cream, grated Parmesan cheese, sea salt, and pepper.

Corn & Chicken Chowder

A simple soup that's good for the soul.

Serves 4

6 cups chicken broth
1 pound skinless, boneless chicken breast halves, thinly sliced
1 can (14.5 ounces) cream-style corn
4 eggs, lightly beaten

In a large saucepan, bring the broth to a boil. Add the chicken, reduce to a simmer, and cook for 3 minutes. Add the corn and simmer for 8 minutes. Whisk in the eggs and cook, stirring, until the eggs separate and spread evenly throughout the soup. Season with sea salt and pepper to taste.

Optional: Add slices of scallion (green onion) to garnish.

Country Italian Sausage Stew

Serves 4

    1 package (12 ounces) lean Italian sausage (try chicken or turkey)
    1 can (15 ounces) butter beans, drained and rinsed
    1 jar (24 ounces) your favorite spicy pasta sauce
    10 ounces potatoes, peeled and chopped

In a nonstick saucepan, lightly brown the sausages. Add the remaining ingredients and cook over medium heat for 45 minutes, or until the potatoes are nice and tender.

Optional: Serve with toasted sourdough and a drizzle of olive oil. A garnish of watercress leaves is lovely, too!

French Onion Soup

The blend of buttery onions and thyme will have them running back for seconds—and thirds.

Serves 4

4 tablespoons (½ stick) butter
6 large onions, thinly sliced
2 teaspoons chopped fresh thyme
6 cups beef broth

In a deep pot, melt the butter over medium-high heat. Just as it begins to brown, add the onions. When all the onions are in the pot, season with pepper and the thyme. Cook, stirring frequently, until the onions are tender, sweet, and a lovely caramel color, about 15 minutes. Add the broth and cover the pot to bring up to a quick boil. Reduce to a simmer and cook for 15 minutes. Ladle the soup into 4 small, deep soup bowls and serve.

Optional: Broil some aged Cheddar or other sharp cheese onto thick slices of French bread and place in the middle of the soup before serving.

Irish Stew

This looks simple, but the flavor in this stew is deliciously complex.

Serves 6

> 2 pounds lamb shoulder chops
> 3 large onions, sliced
> 2 pounds potatoes, peeled and sliced
> 3 tablespoons Worcestershire sauce

Preheat the oven to 325°F. Arrange a layer of chops in a Dutch oven. Season with sea salt and pepper to taste. Cover with a layer of onions and then potatoes. Repeat until all are used. Sprinkle the Worcestershire sauce over the top, then pour in enough water to come two-thirds up the sides. Place on the stovetop and bring to a boil. Cover, transfer to the oven, and bake for 2½ hours, until nice and tender.

Optional: You can use beef broth instead of water. Add whatever veggies you have in the fridge.

Leek & Potato Soup

A lusciously thick soup made all the better with lightly fried "leek chips."

Serves 4

3 tablespoons butter
4 leeks, white and light green parts, chopped
¾ pound potatoes, peeled and diced
1 box (32 ounces) chicken broth

In a saucepan, melt half the butter over low heat. Add the leeks and cook, stirring occasionally, until softened, about 5 minutes. Add the potatoes and cook for 3 minutes. Increase the heat to medium, pour in the broth, and bring to a boil. Reduce to a simmer, cover, and cook until the leeks and potatoes are tender, 35 to 40 minutes. Remove the pan from the heat and add the remaining 1½ tablespoons butter in small pieces, stirring until it's all incorporated. Season with sea salt and pepper to taste. Transfer to a blender and puree until smooth. Serve in warm bowls.

Optional: Serve with "leek chips." Thinly slice some of the trimmed leek greens.
Shallow-fry in hot oil until golden and serve alongside the soup instead of croutons.

Red Pepper & Chorizo Soup

Serves 6

    2 fully cooked chorizo sausages, diced
    4 red bell peppers, diced
    1 can (14.5 ounces) tomatoes
    3 cups chicken broth

In a nonstick saucepan, cook the chorizo for 5 minutes. Remove from the pan and set aside. Add the peppers to the chorizo juices in the pan and cook for 5 minutes. Stir in the tomatoes, season with sea salt and pepper to taste, add the broth, and bring to a boil. Reduce to a simmer and cook until the peppers are tender. Transfer the soup to a blender and puree until smooth. Serve topped with the chorizo pieces.

Salmon & Asparagus Soup

f *Recipe from Alexis Wallis, who wrote: "This is the perfect dish for entertaining . . . really flavorsome with very little effort."*

Serves 4

> 1 pouch or can (5 ounces) red salmon
> 1 can (10.75 ounces) condensed cream of asparagus soup
> 1 cup light cream

Drain the salmon, removing the skin and bones. Puree the salmon (and any juices) in a blender and transfer to a saucepan. Add the soup, cream, and 1 cup water. Gently heat without boiling. Season with pepper, if desired.

Optional: Sprinkle with dill to serve.

Thai Squash Soup

This soup is THAI-RIFIC!!

Serves 4

2 pounds butternut squash, peeled and diced
2 tablespoons red curry paste
1 can (13 ounces) coconut milk
¼ cup chopped cilantro

In a saucepan, cook the squash and red curry paste until it starts to stick. Add the coconut milk and top with enough water to come level with the squash and bring to a boil. Reduce to a simmer and cook until the squash is soft and mushy. Transfer to a blender and puree until smooth. Season with sea salt and pepper to taste and fold in the cilantro.

Tips: You can save time by using canned pumpkin: In a saucepan, combine 1 can (29 ounces) pure pumpkin with the curry paste and coconut milk. Simmer briefly, season, and add the cilantro. Red curry paste, a Thai ingredient, can be found in the Asian foods section.

Tomato & Thyme Soup

This is a soup to warm your hands and your hearts!

Serves 4

16 plum tomatoes, halved lengthwise
2 tablespoons extra virgin olive oil
Leaves from 4 sprigs thyme
1 box (32 ounces) vegetable broth

Preheat the oven to 350°F. Place the tomatoes on a baking sheet cut side up and drizzle with the oil. Sprinkle with the thyme and sea salt and pepper to taste. Bake for 40 minutes, until soft and lightly browned. Remove and let cool slightly. Transfer to a large pot, add the broth, bring to a simmer, and cook for 15 minutes. Use a handheld blender to puree right in the pot (or transfer to a blender). Serve warm.

Optional: Serve with fresh, crusty bread and sprinkled with thyme leaves.

Pizza, Pies & Pasta

Your family and friends are bound to love the sensationally simple recipes within this chapter.

A Tuscan Love Story

I first tasted this divinely rich and delicious sauce at the Galuten household in Los Angeles. I was absolutely amazed to learn it could be made with just four simple ingredients. Many thanks, MG; without your invitation to dinner, I never would have discovered it!

Serves 6

2 cans (28 ounces each) whole peeled tomatoes
½ pound (2 sticks) butter
4 onions, peeled and quartered
1 pound fresh linguine

In a large pot, combine the tomatoes, butter, and onions and bring to a gentle boil. Reduce the heat and simmer for at least 2 hours, allowing time for the delicious flavors to develop. Transfer the sauce to a large bowl and keep warm. Rinse the pot, fill it with salted water, and bring to a boil. Add the linguine and cook for 6 to 8 minutes, or until al dente. Drain, rinse, and stir gently into the sauce, or place the linguine on serving plates and spoon the deliciously flavorful sauce over the pasta.

Tip: To quickly peel onions for any dish, place the onions in a large bowl. Pour boiling water over them and let stand for 5 minutes. Drain and simply rub to remove the skins.

Avocado & Prosciutto Pasta

Serves 4

    1 pound ruffled or spiral pasta
    8 ounces prosciutto, shredded
    1 ripe avocado, cubed
    ¼ cup chili oil, or to taste

In a large pot of boiling salted water, cook the pasta according to package directions. Drain and toss with the remaining ingredients. Pour into a serving bowl and enjoy!

Optional: Instead of prosciutto, try this with ¼ pound diced cooked shrimp.

Tip: Chili oil can easily be replaced with olive oil if you don't want it so spicy.

Chicken Potpie

This redefines fast and fabulous!

Serves 4 to 6

2 sheets frozen puff pastry, thawed
1 can (10.75 ounces) condensed cream of chicken soup
½ rotisserie chicken (about 1 pound), skin and bones discarded, meat cubed
1 bag (19 ounces) frozen mixed vegetables, thawed and drained

Preheat the oven to 350°F. Line a 9-inch baking dish with parchment paper and then one sheet of pastry. In a bowl, combine the soup, chicken, and veggies. Season with sea salt and pepper to taste. Pour the mixture into the bottom crust and cover with the remaining pastry; seal the edges with a fork and cut off the excess pastry. Cut a few vent holes in the top crust and bake until golden brown, about 35 to 40 minutes.

Optional: Brush with beaten egg and sprinkle with poppy seeds and sesame seeds for a really beautiful finish.

Creamy Pesto Chicken Fettuccine

This dish is just lovely and often requested by my kids.

Serves 4

1 pound spinach fettuccine
1 pound skinless, boneless chicken breast halves, chopped
1¼ cups heavy cream
¼ cup prepared basil pesto

In a large pot of boiling salted water, cook the fettuccine according to package directions. Meanwhile, in a nonstick skillet, cook the chicken until golden. Stir in the cream and basil pesto and simmer for 4 to 5 minutes. Add the fettuccine, mix well, and serve warm.

Optional: Sprinkle with chopped fresh basil or Parmesan cheese to serve.

Deep Pan Pizza

I'm always on the lookout for fabulous pizza recipes, so you can imagine my surprise when this was shared on my Facebook page and then my absolute delight when it worked! Happy days!

Serves 4

1 cup self-rising flour
2 tablespoons olive oil
½ cup pizza sauce
4 ounces mozzarella cheese, thinly sliced

In a large, greased nonstick skillet, mix together the flour and oil with ⅔ cup water and a good pinch of salt. It will appear very sticky, so simply work it around the bottom of the pan to spread out into a nice dough. Spoon the pizza sauce onto the dough and spread to cover. Arrange the cheese on top, then season with sea salt and pepper. Cover with a lid and cook over medium heat for 10 minutes. Carefully slide the pizza out onto a cutting board. Let it sit for 2 minutes to cool before cutting it into wedges to serve.

Optional: Sprinkle with fresh basil leaves to serve. This is also nice with a variety of toppings. I had some cherry tomatoes in the fridge, which I halved and added before cooking. If you like your food spicy, add a small pinch of red pepper flakes to the dough.

Gnocchi with Sage & Blue Cheese

A simple but decadent dish that will impress your family and friends.

Serves 4

> 1 package (16 ounces) fresh potato gnocchi
> 4 tablespoons (½ stick) butter
> 2 ounces Cambozola cheese, thinly sliced
> Leaves from 4 sprigs fresh sage

In a large pot of boiling salted water, cook the gnocchi according to package directions. Drain and let sit in the colander. Wipe the pot clean and melt the butter and cheese with the sage. Return the gnocchi to the pot and toss well to coat. Season and serve.

Optional: Top with freshly grated Parmesan cheese.

Maltese Cheese Pie

With four simple ingredients, this pie is really quite amazing.

Serves 4 to 6

3 eggs
1 container (15 ounces) ricotta cheese
¼ cup chopped parsley
2 sheets frozen puff pastry, thawed

Preheat the oven to 350°F. Line an 8-inch round baking dish with parchment paper. In a bowl, beat the eggs; set aside a small amount to paint the top of the pie. Stir the ricotta and parsley into the eggs. Season with sea salt and pepper to taste. Line the baking dish with 1 sheet of the pastry. Pour in the ricotta mixture and cover with the remaining pastry; seal the edges with a fork and trim the excess pastry. Brush the top crust with the reserved egg and cut 2 or 3 vent holes. Bake until the pastry is golden on top, 35 to 40 minutes.

Optional: When baking this I always take the excess pastry pieces, combine them, and roll them out into one flat sheet. Then I use a small heart-shaped cookie cutter to cut out hearts. I dot them on top of the pie: one for each of my three boys, my husband, my dog, and my chicken!

Spaghetti with Parsley & Parmesan

The perfect quick and easy pasta!

Serves 4

> 1 pound spaghetti
> 12 tablespoons (1½ sticks) butter
> 5 tablespoons chopped parsley
> 2 cups grated Parmesan cheese (8 ounces)

In a large pot of boiling salted water, cook the spaghetti according to package instructions. Drain and return to the pot over low heat. Add the butter, parsley, and half the Parmesan and toss well, until the butter and cheese have melted and distributed nicely. Serve immediately, sprinkled with the remaining Parmesan.

Sweet Treats

I have a real sweet tooth.

It's a joy to share some of my family's and friends' favorites with you here!

Apple Crumble

A wonderful recipe that my Aunt Lorraine made for our families a couple of Easters ago. It is really easy and incredibly flavorful.

Serves 6

8 tablespoons (1 stick) butter, melted
2 cans (21 ounces each) apple pie filling
½ cup raisins
1 package (7 ounces) shortbread cookies, crushed

Preheat the oven to 350°F. Lightly grease an 8- or 9-inch baking dish with a little of the butter. Spoon in the apples and sprinkle with the raisins. In a large bowl, mix together the cookie crumbs and the remaining melted butter. Spread the crumbs evenly over the apples and raisins. Bake for 15 to 20 minutes, until the topping is lovely and golden.

Optional: Add a little cinnamon to the crumb mixture, if desired.

Apricot Custard Vol-au-Vents

Serves 6

6 frozen puff pastry shells, thawed
1½ cups prepared vanilla pudding
6 canned apricot halves, drained well and cut in half
¼ cup sliced almonds, toasted

Preheat the oven to 350°F. Line a baking sheet with parchment paper. Place the pastry shells on the baking sheet and bake until crisp, about 5 minutes. Remove from the oven, cool, and fill each with ¼ cup pudding. Top with 2 pieces of apricot and some slivered almonds before serving.

Optional: Serve drizzled with honey.

Baby Banoffees

Baby Banoffees, as my family calls these, are a simple sweet treat that everyone loves.

Serves 12

12 soft ginger cookies
1 can (13.4 ounces) dulce de leche
1 cup whipped cream or whipped topping
1 banana, sliced

Preheat the oven to 325°F. Flip over a muffin pan and place the cookies over the cups. Bake for 5 to 6 minutes to soften the cookies. Flip the pan right side up. While the cookies are still warm and pliable, press them gently into the cups to mold. Divide the dulce de leche evenly among the cookies and top with a spoon of whipped cream and a banana slice.

Baked Rice Pudding

Grandma's classic.

Serves 4

⅓ cup rice, cooked with ⅔ cup water until just done
¾ cup sweetened condensed milk
3 eggs, lightly beaten
¼ cup raisins

Preheat the oven to 350ºF. In a bowl, stir together the rice, condensed milk, 1¾ cups water, the eggs, and raisins. Pour into a 1-quart baking dish. Place the dish in a larger dish with enough hot water to come halfway up the sides of the shallow dish. Bake until set, about 40 minutes.

Optional: Before baking, sprinkle with grated nutmeg.

Banana Bread

One of the world's most popular recipes, it took me sixteen attempts to perfect . . . but I did it!

Serves 8

> 2 large, really ripe bananas
> ½ cup superfine sugar
> 1 cup mayonnaise
> 2 cups self-rising flour

Preheat the oven to 350°F. Line an 8-inch loaf pan with parchment paper. In a medium bowl, mash the bananas. Stir in the sugar. Add the mayonnaise, flour, and a pinch of sea salt and lightly mix until just combined. Pour the batter into the pan. Bake until a skewer inserted into the center comes out clean, 50 minutes. Let cool in the pan for 10 minutes, then turn onto a rack. Enjoy it warm straight from the oven or lightly toasted.

Optional: Add 2 tablespoons maple syrup when mixing the bananas and sugar.

Tip: You can toast the bread—it's yummy served with a little butter or crème fraîche and berries.

Caramel Scrolls

Makes 12 rolls

½ can (13.4-ounce can) dulce de leche
1 sheet frozen puff pastry, thawed
½ cup raisins

Preheat the oven to 350°F. Line a baking sheet with parchment paper. Lay out the pastry on a work surface, then spread the dulce de leche over the pastry. Sprinkle evenly with the raisins. Roll up tightly, starting at a long edge, then cut crosswise into 1¼-inch-thick rolls. Place the scrolls, cut side up, on the baking sheet, allowing room for spreading. Bake until golden brown, 20 to 25 minutes. Transfer to a rack to cool.

Tip: If the pastry roll is a bit too soft to cut, pop it into the freezer for 15 minutes to firm up.

Chocolate Grapes

These are a visual delight and will draw attention at any gathering.

Serves 4

1 bunch (14 ounces) seedless grapes, on the stem
10 ounces dark chocolate, broken up
½ teaspoon canola oil

Line a baking sheet with parchment paper. Wash and thoroughly dry the grapes and let sit at room temperature. In a large microwave-safe bowl, melt the chocolate in 30-second increments, stirring well after each, until nice and smooth. Stir the oil into the chocolate to thin. Add the grapes to the bowl of chocolate, and using a measuring cup, scoop up the chocolate and pour over the top of the grapes for full, even coverage. With a slotted spoon, lift the grapes out of the chocolate, letting the excess drip back into the bowl. Place the grapes on the lined baking sheet and chill in the fridge for 20 minutes to set the chocolate.

Optional: Dust with a little powdered sugar.

Tip: Pour any leftover chocolate into a small parchment paper–lined baking dish. Swirl in some peanut butter or sprinkle with crushed nuts or colored sprinkles. Let set, then break into shards.

Key Lime Pie

Serves 8

4 large egg yolks
1 can (14 ounces) sweetened condensed milk
4 limes, 1 zested and all 4 juiced
1 graham cracker pie crust

Preheat the oven to 300°F. In a bowl, with an electric mixer, beat the egg yolks until they are thick and pale yellow. Turn the mixer off and add the condensed milk. Turn the speed to low and mix in half the lime juice. Once the juice is incorporated, add the other half of the juice and the lime zest and mix until blended (just a few seconds). Pour the mixture into the crust and bake until set, about 12 minutes.

Optional: Serve with whipped cream or lightly dusted with powdered sugar.

Tip: Use the leftover egg whites for a meringue topping. Just before you place the pie in the oven, beat the egg whites with clean beaters until they start to foam. Gradually add ½ cup superfine sugar and beat until a glossy meringue forms. Top the pie with the meringue, making sure to spread it all the way to the edges of the crust to enclose the filling. The baking time is the same.

Mars Bar Rocky Road

Honestly, I will be in your life for a loooong time with this fast, fabulous, and divinely delicious recipe.

Serves 8

14 ounces milk chocolate, broken up
½ bag (10-ounce bag) marshmallows
1 bag (5 ounces) raspberry gummi candies
2 Mars Bars (2 ounces), chopped

Line a baking sheet with parchment paper. In a large microwave-safe bowl, melt the chocolate in 30-second increments, stirring after each, until nice and smooth. Let cool slightly before stirring in the remaining ingredients. Toss to coat. Spoon the mixture evenly onto the baking sheet and refrigerate for 40 minutes. Cut into squares to serve.

Tip: This works well with Milky Ways as well. In Australia, pink marshmallows come in the same bag along with white ones!

Ooey-Gooey Chocolate Puddings

The name says it all!

Serves 4

> 1 bar (3 ounces) dark chocolate, chopped
> 8 tablespoons (1 stick) butter
> 1 cup chocolate cake mix (see Tip)
> 2 eggs, lightly beaten

Preheat the oven to 350°F. Melt the chocolate and 7 tablespoons of the butter in the microwave or in a saucepan over low heat. Let cool slightly, then stir in the cake mix and eggs and mix well. Grease four 8-ounce ramekins or custard cups well with the remaining 1 tablespoon butter. Dividing evenly, pour the batter into the ramekins. Bake until the tops of the puddings are set, 12 to 14 minutes. Serve in the ramekins or turn out onto individual dessert plates.

Optional: Serve with a dollop of whipped cream or a scoop of vanilla ice cream.

Tip: Store the rest of the cake mix in an airtight container or resealable plastic bag, ready for the next batch of puddings!

Peach Slice

Serves 8

    1 package (15 ounces) vanilla cake mix
    ½ pound (2 sticks) butter, melted
    1 can (14 ounces) sliced peaches, drained
    1½ cups sour cream

Preheat the oven to 350°F. Line a 13 by 9-inch baking dish with parchment paper. In a bowl, combine the cake mix and melted butter to form a dough. Spread the dough evenly in the baking dish and bake for 15 minutes. Meanwhile, combine the peaches and sour cream. Spread evenly over the base and return to the oven for another 15 minutes. Let cool to room temperature, then chill in the fridge (this gives the base time to set). Serve chilled.

Optional: Sprinkle with cinnamon before the final bake. This is equally delicious using 2 peeled, thinly sliced apples instead of the peaches. If peaches are in season, you might want to make your own stewed peaches rather than using canned. In a saucepan, add ¼ cup sugar and ¾ cup water to 1½ pounds of peeled and halved peaches. Bring to a boil over medium heat, then reduce the heat and simmer for 15 minutes.

Scones

The only thing better than the delicious aroma of freshly baked scones is eating them with jam and cream.

Makes 12 scones

> 4 cups self-rising flour
> 1¼ cups heavy cream
> 1 cup 7UP soda

Preheat the oven to 425°F. Line a baking sheet with parchment paper. Sift the flour into a bowl, make a well in the center, and pour in the cream and soda. Mix to make a firm dough. Roll the dough out and cut with a biscuit cutter. Arrange closely together on the baking sheet and bake until golden brown, about 12 minutes.

Optional: Substitute unflavored seltzer for the soda and add some grated sharp cheese, fresh herbs, diced bacon, or chopped sun-dried tomatoes for a delicious, savory scone.

With Thanks

Although I have been collecting recipes, hints, and tips for this book for nearly three years and had a vision for the kind of book I wanted to pull together, it was only possible with the help of some incredibly consistent and supportive people.

Janelle McCosker: Eight months pregnant and you stood for two solid days, cooking, styling, eating (yes, we saw you), and laughing through a grueling photo shoot.

Melanie Roberts: I will never look at a bunch of grapes the same way: check out page 168 to see what I mean. Mel R., you are a choco-genius!

Leonie Wohlsen: The consummate professional, poised and graceful—are these really the qualities of a fine chef?

Kay Gear: You opened your house and let me raid it for elegant plates, beautiful bowls, terrines, vases, and so much more.

Jan Neale: My mother-in-law, who tirelessly washed dishes (then tried to find them again) for two days nonstop and is still talking to me!

Jennette McCosker: The World's BEST MUM. No more needs to be said.

Melinda, Kate, and Michelle: You are my A-Team—just trying to work out which one of us is Mr. T.

Glen Turnbull: Who I'm sure now does own the record for the most trips to a supermarket in a day—although there was a noted four-hour absence on Day 1 . . . how long does 18 holes of golf take?

Every one of you contributed to the look and feel of this beautiful book. Know that what you did is in a format now that will help thousands around the world rediscover the wonders of gloriously easy home-cooked meals.

With love & gratitude,

Kim

Index

hazelnut, in Toasted Nutella Sammies, 16, *17*
Honey-Baked Chicken, 94, *95*
Huevos Rancheros, 6, *7*
Hunia, Shane, 2

I

Indian:
    Chicken Tikka Masala, 64, *65*
    Tandoori Lamb Chops, 84, *85*
ingredients, xii–xiii
Irish Stew, 124, *125*
Italian:
    Bolognese Sauce, 62, *63*
    Chicken Cacciatore, 44, *45*
    Chorizo & Pea Frittata, 24, *25*
    Deep Pan Pizza, 146, *147*
    Sausage Stew, Country, 120, *121*
    see also pasta

J

Jarlsberg & Chicken Casserole, 46, *47*

K

Key Lime Pie, 170, *171*
Kill, Clare, 20

L

lamb:
    Casserole, French, 48, *49*
    Chops, Tandoori, 84, *85*

Irish Stew, 124, *125*
    & Potato Bake, 42
    Roast, 98, *99*
"Lasagna," Roast Beef, 30, *31*
Leek & Potato Soup, 126, *127*
Lemon Butter, 8, *9*
Lime, Key, Pie, 170, *171*
Lobster, Sweet Chili, 82
lunches, *see* snacks & lunches

M

Macaroni Bake, 96, *97*
Maltese Cheese Pie, 150, *151*
Mars Bar Rocky Road, 172, *173*
marshmallows, in Mars Bar Rocky Road, 172, *173*
meringue topping, with leftover egg whites, 170
milk, in Strawberry Muesli Smoothie, 14, *15*
mozzarella cheese:
    Chicken Enchilada Cake, 88, *89*
    Chorizo & Pea Frittata, 24, *25*
    Deep Pan Pizza, 146, *147*
Muesli Strawberry Smoothie, 14, *15*
mushrooms:
    Beef Stroganoff, 58, *59*
    7-Minute Risotto, 40
Mussels in White Wine, 74, *75*

N

noodles:
    Yummy Tuna Bake, 110, *111*
    see also pasta
Nutella Sammies, Toasted, 16, *17*

INVITATION

Join our Foodie Family

At 4 Ingredients we cultivate a family of busy people all bound together by the desire to create good, healthy, homemade meals quickly, easily, and economically. Our aim is to save us all precious time and money in the kitchen. If this is you, too, then we invite you to join our growing family where we share kitchen wisdom daily. If you have a favorite recipe, or a tip that has worked for you in your kitchen and you think others would enjoy it, please contact us at:

facebook.com/4ingredientspage

You Tube 4 Ingredients Channel

4ingredients.com.au

@4ingredients

Happy entertaining!

Kim